MW00582754

THE ART OF PETAR MESELDŽIJA

UNLIMITED IMAGINATION

DARK DRAGON BOOKS

WWW.DARKDRAGONBOOKS.COM

DARK DRAGON BOOKS *Art* COLLECTION

Dedicated to my dear parents, Vera and Stanimir Meseldžija.

P.M.

A special thanks to: Dragan Bibin, Dragan Polovina, Ryan Bongers, Gregory Manchess, Ivan Kampel, John Fleskes, Amin Gemei, Dejan Nenadov, Marcel Salome and, last but not least, my wife Anita.

Edited and designed by:
PETAR MESELDŽIJA

Cover design by:
PETAR MESELDŽIJA AND DRAGAN BIBIN

Book design assistance:
DRAGAN BIBIN

Publisher:
AMIN GEMEI

ISBN: 978-94-6078-235-3

WWW.PETARMESELDZIJAART.COM
WWW.FACEBOOK.COM/THEARTOFPETARMESELDZIJA
WWW.DARKDRAGONBOOKS.COM
WWW.FACEBOOK.COM/DARKDRAGONBOOKS

All art in this book is copyright © 2013 Petar Meseldžija, except where noted. Text and design copyright © 2013 Petar Meseldžija. Text on page 5 copyright © 2013 Gregory Manchess.

This edition copyright © 2013 Petar Meseldžija & Dark Dragon Books, Breda.

Illustrations on pages 95, 97, 98, 99, 101, 102, 103, 105, 106, 109, 111 copyright © 2013 Scholastic, Inc..

All rights reserved. No parts of this book may be reproduced, stored in any retrieval system, or transmitted in any other form, or by any means, electronic, mechanical, photocopying, or otherwise without prior permission in writing by the copyright holder(s).

The ART of PETAR MESELDŽIJA

Self portrait, 1987

The Art of Petar Meseldžija

by Gregory Manchess

I already love this book. So many art books suffer from the verbose, banal descriptions of the very image the reader has before them, as if the picture must first be explained before the viewer can understand it.

Petar Meseldžija's work is far too good, far beyond mere technical description, to reduce it to intellectual banter. His paintings must be felt, allowed to draw one in, pull one from the everyday. As with any skilled painter, the pieces work on multiple levels, beyond mere description. He gets to me through the paint itself. He is an artist's artist, a painter's painter.

Meseldžija's pictures are fairly alive with nature, enhanced by an observation of reality that pours over with emotive paint application. The strokes have life, from the first bottom layers up through the value ranges and into the top layers of pigment. And wow, those top layers are exquisite.

Study the dance of the strokes across the entire surface of his works. Notice how the brush works to define the shape without the labor, how each layer supports the one above, how they allow every passage to inform and thrill.

Petar resists the temptation to render without thought, to drift into reportage. Even metal has animation, whether soundly structured or in the shimmer of light. Everything has life--from nature, to action, to strokes--nothing stagnant, nothing a struggle, nothing overworked.

Anyone can tell, Petar's figures are breathtaking, wrapped in animated fabric in lugubrious folds that mimic sinuous flesh. Anatomy so accurate he appears, at will, to blatantly leave every proportion behind, as he does with his beasts and woeful ogres, and still have you believe the character is intact, its life complete.

Even Petar's trees have character. Branches designed to move, supported by rocks that live in a motion-filled world where the wind catches capes like conceptual sculptures. They are statements, signs not only of animation, but of the life he captures within inanimate objects.

Still, the mark of an admired painter is inherent within the animals they depict, particularly horses. Meseldžija horses are structured so beautifully they seem aware of the paint that builds them.

Then there's his light control. Understanding light is perhaps the painter's most substantial struggle, the hallmark of a master so easily detected by other painters. I almost wonder if Petar Meseldžija can manipulate light as some clandestine alchemist. Petar's pigment shines as if it generated it's own glow. Observe how the sun transmits its light through the leaves in the painting 'Apple?' (pages 56, 57). The painting could easily dominate any digital piece using tricks like lens flare or crepuscular rays.

I speak highly of the work not to impress, or merely to compliment. This is painting that is matched only by the great paintings across the planet. It deserves a place, and likely will, amongst the history of oil painting, worthy of Saturday afternoon museum attendees staring slack-jawed at the skill and leaving with the same enthusiasm Petar loads into each piece.

This isn't just another oil painter, another painterly approach to realism. This is historical, timeless, generation-inspiring work, the kind that eventually garners thick tomes by professors of classic art study. This is the level that all artists shoot for in their paint, whether it's detailed, painterly, or abstract. Petar handles the pigment as if he was born to it, as if the pigment's potential resides in his brushes for only him to release.

Like the enthusiasm that exudes from each painting, and every drawing, his personality is nearly the same. An honest curiosity for people and life effervesces from his discussions about painting. Together, with passion and a vision so distinct, Meseldžija's work will inspire and drive future painters to mimic his skill, his life, his energetic depictions. They will be hard pressed to equal it. Only so many can achieve an endeavor so clearly stated.

My own work is already absorbing his infectious expression.

Krampi, 1981

From comics to painting

by Petar Meseldžija

On August 5th 1965, at ten minutes past four in the morning, a little bundle of flesh and bone, as pink as a piglet, drew a deep breath and released its first cry, announcing his arrival to this world. There was no new star alight in the skies above Novi Sad at the time of my birth. Millions of souls entered the world that day, and millions have left it since. There was nothing significant in being born at that particular moment and in that particular place. Life threw yet another die and they named it Petar.

My parents were poor, but young and enthusiastic and full of hope that Life would be generous and allow them to fulfill their dreams. They were living in a basement at the time of my arrival; and although they did their best to make it as cozy as possible, it remained cold and damp. My grandfather visited us at the beginning of my first winter, and upon seeing the poor situation in which we were living, said to my parents: "This child is going to die here. I shall take him home with me. His grandmother and I will look after him until you are able to provide better living conditions." Wanting the best for their child, my parents agreed.

I lived for some years with my grandparents in the village, while my parents came to visit me on the weekends. Growing up in the countryside was a blessing that shaped the contours of my personality as well as the artist within me. I spent my first few summers barefoot, absorbing all the love and generosity Mother Earth had to offer. I felt her directly through her elements, even

tasted her soil, and found that she was delicious! It was there and then, that I fell in love with Life.

Outside our village, just over the hill, rolls the mighty Danube river (Dunav in Serbian) meandering slowly and self-confidently along the base of the Fruška Gora mountain on its way to the Black Sea. This majestic river which - according to Slavic legend - was formed from the blood of the ancient hero Dunai, was my playground. These waters have entered my blood and never left me: the river still flows in my veins, acting as a medium connecting me to the epic dimensions of the land from which I sprang, and helping me to reflect its pulse in my art.

My childhood was a wonderful adventure. I had many good friends, both boys and girls, as well as animals and trees, but the greatest friend of all was my uncle. He taught me those things which a village boy must know: how to play games, how to catch a fly with your bare hands, how to fish, how to make a bow-and-arrow, and a sling and a flute. However the most precious thing that I gained from my uncle was the love of comics. He was a devoted reader of comic books and he introduced them to me. In doing so, my uncle unknowingly brought Art directly into my hands and into my life, thus awakening my vocation.

Comics were my first love. I was truly infatuated. It was a passion that would last for more than two decades. I loved everything about them, even the smell of their pages. I still remember vividly the little newspaper kiosk on the corner of the street where I used to buy comic books. This kiosk was my shrine, the altar of my temple.

At the beginning of the eighties, when I began drawing comics more seriously, the market for comic books in Serbia was already well developed. A few large publishing companies offered a healthy and reliable podium for emerging artistic talent. The most vital, exciting and enduring of all was Marketprint, from Novi Sad, the publisher of the legendary Stripoteka, the best comic magazine in the country.

My art career officially started on June 6th 1981 when the first three strips of my comic series Krampi were published in Stripoteka, issue 654. I will never forget how I felt when I saw it in print. Like a prehistoric hunter encountering the phenomenal depictions of the animals on the walls of a cave, I was overwhelmed. It was a truly magical, life-changing experience.

During the subsequent years I spent a significant portion of my life drawing comics, creating about 300 pages. I was as happy as one could be! But as the time passed, my appetite for artistic expression increased. I still enjoyed drawing comics, but the artistic spirit in me - eager to break through certain creative boundaries and discover what lies beyond -

Drawing from the second episode of comic *Esmeralda*, 1986. The first episode was never published and the whereabouts of the original pages are unknown.

brought me to the Art Academy. From the mid-eighties the object of my artistic focus began to shift from comics to painting. Colors started to play a more dominant role in my life, and the rich smell of oil paint replaced the smell of comic books. My new artistic aspirations were high: I wanted to be able to paint objects in such a convincing way that the pigeons would descend on my canvas, fooled by the realism and illusion of the painted grapes.

Picture from an unfinished comic, 1990

The next four fantastic years were spent studying art and painting; and although I continued drawing comics, the desire to create them - a flame that burned so brightly in the past - started to diminish. It went out definitely in 1992, when I drew the last page of the comic book Kanoo. It was then that I decided to focus all of my creative energy on painting and illustration. I was already living in the Netherlands when I made this decision. Things were pretty tough for me. I lived the life of a poor artist, existing in anonymity, a stranger to Dutch society and desperately struggling to survive. I kept my head above water by concentrating on commercial art, painting many posters and greeting cards, illustrating a book and taking on private commissions of various kinds.

At the end of the nineties, after finishing a stressful and frustrating illustration commission, I chose to abandon commercial art and to focus on the Fine Art painting. As I would later discover, my heart would not give up entirely on illustration, for after a few years of creating "serious" Art, I found myself back on the illustration market painting book covers. In addition to the commissioned work, I continued to work on my own book project The Legend of Steel Bashaw, perhaps my most

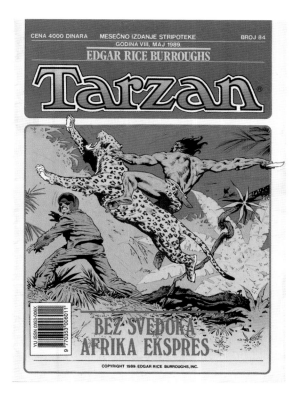

Issue of *Tarzan* comic book with my drawing on the cover, 1989. From 1988 to 1990 I was a member of Marketprint Tarzan team and created 4 episodes, or 64 comic pages of Tarzan.

important artistic creation to date. It was finished in 2008 and published in Serbia that same year. The publication of the U.S. edition, would come out two years later, marking a turning point in my career: my breakthrough

Drawing from the second episode of *Esmeralda,* 1986

Opposite: Comic page from a short story *Dream*, 1984

on the international fantasy art market. Illustration conventions followed, as did lectures, workshops, new book projects, new paintings, more exhibitions, more commissions, more joy... Fortunately, this story continues to unfold.

Now, more than 30 years after the publication of my first comic, I look back on the trail left by my pencils and brushes. During this time, I created numerous imaginary worlds and populated them with various creatures; and although no pigeon descended on my painted grapes, our dog once growled at one of my life-size nude drawings. If I now squint my eyes to blur some mistakes and imperfections, I must

admit that I am quite content with what I see. I am also grateful for having the opportunity to fulfill my dreams and to become the artist I always wanted to be.

From comics to painting, and beyond... What a wonderful journey!

Koog aan de Zaan

28-03-2013

Pages 10 and 11: *Tarzan.* Cover drawing and a page from the episode The Bride of King Bohun, 1988
Tarzan © owned by Edgar Rice Burroughs Inc. and used by permission. All rights reserved.

Pages 12 and 13: From the unpublished comic book *Kanoo*, 1991

This page: Drawings created during my studies at the art academy, 1986 – 1990

Grandmother, 1989

THE ART OF
PETAR MESELDŽIJA

Posters

In 1993, I had the opportunity to work with Verkerke Reproducties, a Dutch poster company, at that time one of the biggest in the world. The poster business was booming, and a good poster artist was sought after and well paid. In those days, as a starving artist, I welcomed any chance to work, and was very happy and excited when I received my first poster assignment from such a successful and reliable company.

During the next 7 years, I painted about 120 posters and greeting cards. Working for Verkerke was extremely important for me, not only because I was receiving work on a regular basis - which enabled me to earn a relatively stable living - but also because it offered me a training period, or kind of apprenticeship. While working on posters, I learned many useful things about the business of commercial art, developed my painting skills, and deepened my artistic insights.

Trio Clownesque. 50x60 cm, oil on canvas on board, 1993

Noah's Ark. 70x100 cm, oil on board, 1994

Dinosaurs.
70x125 cm, oil on
canvas, 1993

Serenade. 20x27 cm, watercolor on paper, 1993

Clown and dog. 50x70 cm, oil on canvas on board, 1993

Squirrel Christmas. 22x33 cm, oil on paper, 1991

All Creatures, Great and Small.
70x100 cm, oil on board,
1994

Snow White 3.
Oil on cardboard, 1997

Books

Books have always been an important aspect of my life. Ever since I can remember, I have been reading, collecting, illustrating and even writing them. It all started a long time ago when I first fell in love with comics. Later, after being introduced to books on the art of Frank Frazetta, and especially after seeing the legendary book Fairies, created by Alan Lee and Brian Froud, my attention shifted towards illustration and illustrated books. I then began dreaming of becoming a book illustrator.

Books of all kinds have passed through my hands since then, some leaving a profound and lasting impression on me and my work. They not only brought me infinite joy and inspiration, they also helped me to find my own path and infused my Art with substance and meaning.

Below: One of 9 illustrations from my first illustrated book Peter Enkork (*Jack One-Step*), by Terry Jones. 26x26 cm, watercolor on paper, 1990, published by Mladinska Knjiga, Slovenia.

Above: *Giant and Bobo.*
35x50 cm, watercolor on paper, 1989/1990

From *Peter Enkorak*.
26x26 cm, watercolor on
paper, 1990

Unfinished illustration.
32,5x39,5 cm, watercolor on
paper, 1994

From *Peter Enkorak*.
26x26 cm, watercolor on
paper, 1990

Opposite: *Igraine.* From *King Arthur and the Knights of the Round Table,* 22x30 cm, oil on paper, 1999, published by Grimm Press, Taiwan.

The Duel. From *King Arthur and the Knights of the Round* Table, 22x43,5 cm, acrylic on paper, 1999

Merlin. From *King Arthur and the Knights of the Round Table,* 22x15 cm, oil on paper, 1999

Guinevere's rescue. From
*King Arthur and the
Knights of the Round
Table,*
22x43,5 cm, acrylic on
paper, 1999

The Golden Apple-tree and the Nine Peahens. Illustration from the book *Serbian Folktales*, 32x50 cm, oil on panel, 2012, published by Čarobna Knjiga, Serbia.

The world of fairy tales, legends and mythology has always attracted me. Tales that deal with imaginary realms have been the source of inspiration for many of my paintings. I cannot deny that this fascination with the fantastic and the imaginary might also entail some escapist tendencies, but I believe the main reason for this attraction involves a genuine interest in the language of symbols, archetypes and metaphors that make up the fabric of these "other" worlds. Realms of the imaginary not only serve to reflect beliefs, struggles and aspirations of our ancestors in ancient times; they also suggest a greater, more universal truth of the human condition, quite contrary to the partial truths which are offered to us in contemporary culture and mainstream art.

Above and left:
Preliminary drawings for the illustrations from *The Golden Apple-tree and the Nine Peahens.*
Pencil on paper, 2012

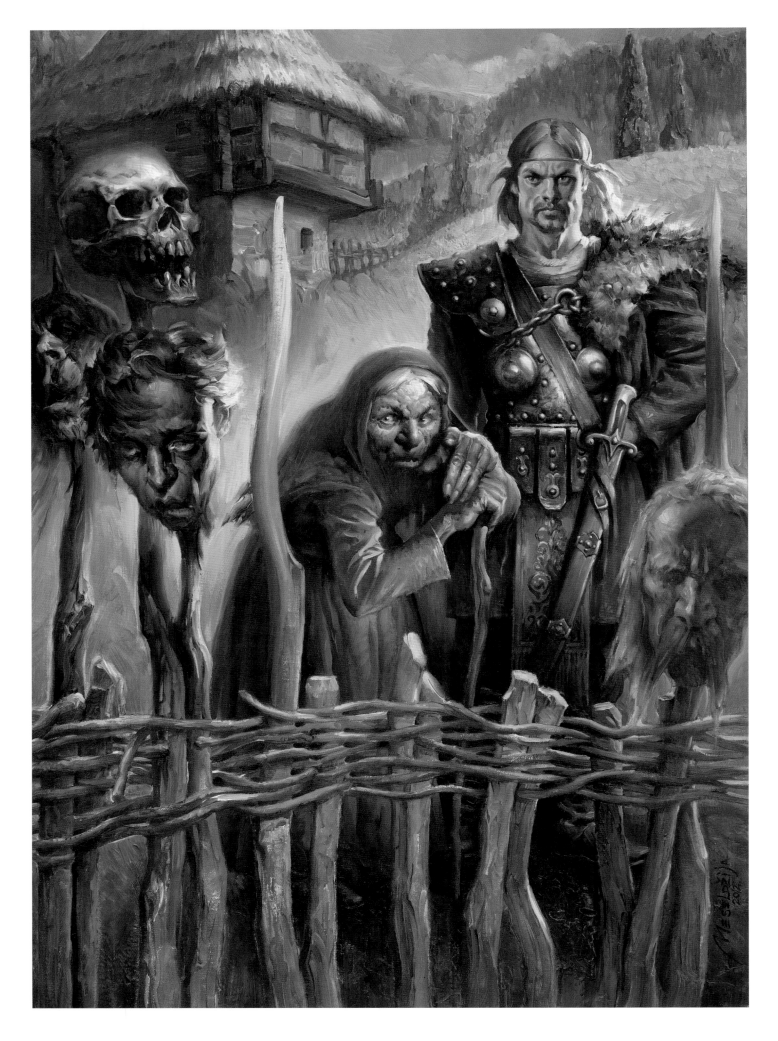

Opposite: *The Golden Apple-tree and the Nine Peahens.* 36x50 cm, oil on panel, 2012

One of several preliminary sketches for the painting on the opposite page. Pencil on paper, 2012

Final preliminary drawing for the same illustration. Pencil on paper, 2012

The Golden Apple-tree and the Nine Peahens.
48X72 cm, oil on panel, 2012

Preliminary drawing, pencil on paper, 2010

Knight and Dwarfs.
From the book *Banished Creatures– Serbian Mythology,* by Milenko Bodirogić,
32x58 cm, oil on Masonite, 2010, published by Orfelin Izdavaštvo, Serbia.

⊸•————⧉⟩ BOOKS

Giants – The Fighting Bulls. From *Banished Creatures – Serbian Mythology,*
oil on Masonite, 55x90 cm, 2010

This is a preliminary drawing for the painting, Giants: The Fighting Bulls, created for a book on Serbian mythology called Banished Demons. The painting shows a group of giants amusing themselves by watching two bulls fighting. This piece is inspired by a famous painting, The Cock Fight, by Paja Jovanović, one of the

greatest Serbian masters from 19th/20th century.

I started to draw on a relatively small sheet of paper, but the sketch progressed well and soon grew into a detailed preliminary drawing. In order to accommodate the growing composition, I needed to add another two sheets of paper to the initial drawing.

Preliminary drawing for
Giants – The Fighting Bull.
Pencil on paper, 2010

Tyrael battling against Tal Rash. **From** *Diablo III: Book of Cain,*
pencil on paper, 2011. Copyright © 2013 Blizzard Entertainment, Inc.

Gottfried Teutonicu. From *Banished Demons – Serbian Mythology,*
pencil on colored paper, 2010

Pretty Tralja (Lepi Tralja).
Pencil on paper, 2010

Frightened Monster.
13x17,5 cm, oil on panel, 2013

Girl riding a giant.
Pen, brush and ink on paper, 2012

When I asked the client who commissioned this drawing whether he had a particular theme on his mind, he said: "I like the idea of a tree, a giant battling a valiant king and a beautiful woman." A few days later, after presenting him with the finished drawing, he commented: " That is why you are the artist. I say, tree, giant, noble hero and girl and then you create a splendid adventure scene! And you get a horse in there, too!"

Unk!
Pencil on paper, 2010

Not all giants are ugly!

Not all giants are ugly.
Pencil on colored paper, 2011

Giants.
Pencil on paper, 2011

Pages from a sketchbook, pencil on paper, 2001

Giant and girl. Pencil, pen, brush and ink on paper, 2012

I always loved to draw giants and ogres. Not only wonderfully grotesque and fascinating subjects, these creatures are also inspiring as symbols. I see them as the embodiment of a deep-rooted, untamed and intuitive side of human nature. The long and painful process of cultivating human society has produced great civilizations, but often deprived human beings of their spontaneity and unrestrained expression, removing them further away from Life in its purest form.

Preliminary drawing of a giant from *The Legend of Steel Bashaw*.
Pencil on paper, 2003

Giantess.
Pencil on paper, 2010

Right:
Svjatogor.
Preliminary drawing,
pencil on paper, 2010

Lower right:
*Svjatogor – The protector
of the mountains.*
Pencil, pen, brush and
ink on paper, 2012

Lower left:
Giant.
Pencil on paper, 2010

Svjatogor.
27x56 cm, oil on
panel, 2010

Apple?
50x65 cm, oil on panel,
2009

Hans and Greta.
50x90 cm, oil on panel,
2009

My paternal grandmother and me in Pribelja village. Photo, 1969

Upper right:
Baba Dojda.
Oil and pencil on paper, 2010

Below:
Detail from
Hans and Greta.

The drawing above features Baba Dojda, a friendly dwarf medicine woman, who is in fact this character's second incarnation. She was first conceived as a preliminary drawing for the evil witch from a painting of Hans and Greta. During one of my visits to my parents' home in Serbia, I showed the reproduction of the finished painting to my father, explaining that I used an old photo of grandmother as inspiration.

He looked at the picture for a while and, recognizing the characteristic posture of his deceased mother, said angrily: "Shame on you, my son! You have made a witch of my mother!". I was a bit shocked but also pleased by his announcement. It was the first time my father responded emotionally to one of my paintings.

Real trouble cannot be hidden 1.
Illustration from the book *Serbian Folktales,* 22x33 cm, oil on paper, 2008

Real trouble cannot be hidden 2.
50X80 cm, oil on panel,
2008 - 2012

Opposite:
The Legend of Steel Bashaw 9.
50x70 cm, oil on Masonite,
2001. The book *The Legend
of Steel Bashaw* was initially
published in Serbia in
2008 by Zmaj. Published
in the U.S. in 2010 by Flesk
Publications.

Above and left:
Details from
The legend of Steel Bashaw 9

The Legend of Steel Bashaw 4. 70x100 cm, oil on Masonite, 2003

Details from
*The Legend of Steel
Bashaw 4*

Detail from
The Legend of Steel Bashaw 4

In November 1993, after working on commercial projects for two years, I felt a strong urge to paint something just for myself. I did not know that this painting would mark the beginning of a long and wondrous journey into the folklore, history and literary heritage of my native country. Nor did I know this journey would eventually end up in the publication of The Legend of Steel Bashaw, a book that would change my life. The Legend of Steel Bashaw is my own retelling of the popular Serbian fairy tale, Baš Čelik. The genesis of this book was long and uncertain, and involved many breaks in production, the longest of which lasted 7 years. All in all, I needed 15 years to complete it. Having been separated for so long from my home and family, for I left my homeland in 1991, I often felt terribly homesick. This intensely personal project, with its roots in my native folklore, offered me a substitute for the actual contact with people and places I left behind. One might say The Legend of Steel Bashaw was conceived out of longing and pain.

Preliminary drawing for *The Legend of Steel Bashaw 5*. Pencil on paper, 2003

The Legend of Steel Bashaw 5. 50x70 cm, oil on Masonite, 2003 - 2006

The Legend of Steel Bashaw 6. 50x70 cm, oil on Masonite, 2003 – 2006

Preliminary drawing for *The Legend of Steel Bashaw 6*. Pencil on paper, 2003

The Legend of Steel-Bashaw 8. 40x60 cm, oil on Masonite, 1993

Preliminary drawing for *The Legend of Steel Bashaw 3.* Pencil, pen and ink on paper, 1994

The Legend of Steel Bashaw 3. 40x60 cm, oil on Masonite, 1994

Above: Detail from
The Legend of Steel Bashaw 3

Right: Detail from the preliminary drawing for
The Legend of Steel Bashaw 16.
Pencil on paper, 2005

In illustrating national folktales, one is inevitably confronted with questions regarding historical and ethnological authenticity. These stories are primarily fictional, but also firmly rooted in a cultural ground, which makes certain features within that culture significant. While it is quite apparent that accuracy plays a fundamental and decisive role in depicting a specific moment in history, it is less evident when dealing with fairy tales or mythology. Since I began to work on The Legend of Steel Bashaw, I have asked myself just how authentic and historically accurate one must be when depicting a fairy tale. Clearly, a certain dose of authenticity is required, but at the same time, one has to be aware that too much history in fairy tale pictures will kill their magic.

The Legend of Steel Bashaw 16. 50x70 cm, oil on Masonite, 2005 – 2008

The Legend of Steel Bashaw 14. 50x70 cm, oil on Masonite, 2008

The Legend of Steel Bashaw 10.
70x100 cm, oil on Masonite, 2003 - 2006

The Legend of Steel Bashaw 11. 60x80 cm, oil on Masonite, 2007

Detail from
*The Legend of
Steel Bashaw 11*

When depicting a character from a specific folktale, it is desirable to show sufficient attributes to suggest the national traits in clothing and physiognomy, but one does not have to be entirely ethnologically accurate. As long as the right direction is indicated and the designs are infused with enough imaginative and evocative material to captivate the reader, the picture will be convincing and the magic preserved. It is all about pointing the "finger" towards the right symbols and contexts, rather than offering a mere reportage.

The Legend of Steel Bashaw 7. 50x70 cm, oil on Masonite, 2007

Preliminary drawing for *The Legend of Steel Bashaw 7*. Pencil on paper, 2007

The Legend of Steel Bashaw 2. 50x70 cm, oil on Masonite, 2008

The Legend of Steel Bashaw 12. 50x65 cm, oil on Masonite, 2008

*The Legend of
Steel Bashaw 13.*
70x100 cm, oil on
Masonite, 2008

Detail from
The Legend of Steel Bashaw 1

The Legend of Steel Bashaw 1. 50x70 cm, oil on Masonite, 2002

Although The Legend of Steel Bashaw takes place in some distant and fictive past, the actual stage on which the tale's epic drama unfolds is Nature. With her various forms, especially the trees, mother Nature provided me with an infinite amount of inspiration and elation – vital ingredients in the process of creating this book. Whether the impenetrable Balkan woods, the graceful hills of Dutch South Limburg, the majestic fells and lakes of Eng-

The Legend of Steel Bashaw 15.
70x100 cm, oil on Masonite,
2003 - 2008

land's Lake District, or the elegant birch forests
of North America, the nature of the Northern
Hemisphere helped transport my mind to an
archetypal level of existence, which served as
the starting point of my tale.

Book Covers

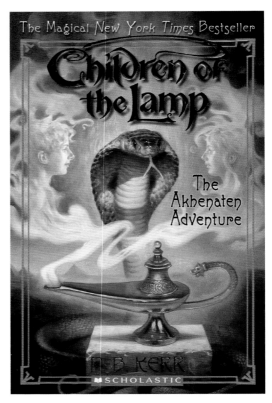

For many years I wanted to paint book covers, but never got the chance to do it, so I eventually put aside the idea of becoming a book cover illustrator.

But at the end of 2004 I was approached by an art director from Scholastic Inc., a U.S. publisher, who asked if I would be interested to make a few book covers for them. I was informed about the conditions of the commission and offered a handsome fee for each cover. Needless to say, I was delighted by this proposal. I had some doubt that I would be able to fulfill the demands of the commission - for this was a new and uncharted territory for me – but I bravely accepted. In the next few years I painted 11 book covers for this publisher.

The cover of *Children of the Lamp*
– The Akhenaten Adventure. This is the first book cover I
did for Scholastic Inc. from the U.S..

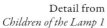

Detail from
Children of the Lamp 1

Children of the Lamp 1. 50x70cm, oil on Masonite, 2004

One of the preliminary
drawings for
Children of the Lamp 2

Detail from
Children of the Lamp 2

◦━━◈◈◈━ BOOK COVERS

Children of the Lamp 2. 50x70 cm, oil on Masonite, 2005

Children of the Lamp 3.
50x65 cm , oil on
Masonite, 2005

While working on the third cover from the Children of the Lamp series by P.B. Kerr, I encountered - for the first time - a form of prudery in publishing. The editors thought that the opening in the Cobra King's skirt was dangerously close to his genitals. So, I was asked to cover up that part of the man's leg, which I did in Photoshop, by pasting a little patch onto the upper area of the opening. When the book was released, however, the main portion of the skirt, including the "problematic" part, was covered by decorative elements as well as the author's name, making my corrections redundant.

Children of the Lamp 5. 50x70 cm , oil on Masonite, 2007

Preliminary drawings for
Children of the Lamp 4.
Pencil on paper 2007

Detail from
Children of the Lamp 4.

According to the publisher, the problem with the preliminary drawing (upper right) of this fourth Children of the Lamp cover was that the boy's bottom was too prominent. They requested that I redraw him in order to make his backside less exposing.

After the painting was finished, the editors then claimed that the boy's torso was a little too short. I corrected that as well and - after the revision was approved – sent the high resolution image of the painting to the publisher. Instead of using this image, however, the publisher mistakenly printed the low resolution image that was made before the requested correction. As a result, the published cover was a little blurry and the boy's torso stayed "short".

Children of the Lamp 4. 42x57 cm, oil on Masonite, 2007

Children of the Lamp 6. 70x100 cm, oil on panel, 2009

The Unicorn Chronicles 4. 44x60 cm, oil on paper on wooden panel, 2009

Preliminary drawing for
The Unicorn Chronicles 3.
Pencil on paper, 2007

Rejected version of the
character from
The Unicorn Chronicles 3.

This is the first of my four covers from the Unicorn Chronicles series by Bruce Coville. The concept for the illustration was quite exciting, so I rented some costumes and props, did a photo-shoot and set down immediately to work.

The preliminary drawing for the composition was refused by the publisher; the second one was approved (top). After about three weeks of intense labor, I finished the piece. The editors loved the way it was painted, but disliked the look of the girl (left). I repainted this poor girl two more times, yet they were still not satisfied. Finally, the editors found and photographed a model with the features they required – her physiognomy was the main issue - and sent me the photos. After the third revision, the painting was finally approved.

The Unicorn Chronicles 3. 50x70 cm, oil on Masonite, 2007

The Unicorn Chronicles 2. 50x70 cm, oil on Masonite, 2008

This is probably my favorite book cover, not because the painting's composition is particularly interesting - for it is one of the least imaginative and dynamic covers of all - but because it is painted elegantly and without any restrain. There are no over-worked parts and the freshness and fluidity of the brush strokes is preserved throughout. The main ingredient which enabled me to achieve these objectives is the highly inspirational photo reference I received from the publisher. Of all the paintings I have created for Scholastic, this is the only one which I intend to keep.

Detail from
The Unicorn Chronicles 2.

Preliminary drawing for *The Unicorn Chronicle 1*. Pencil on paper, 2007

The Unicorn Chronicle 1. 50x70 cm, oil on Masonite, 2007

As far as I am concerned, this is the worst cover I ever painted. It was also the last one I did for Scholastic. Establishing the right composition was a frustrating process, because many of the preliminary drawings were rejected by the publisher. By the time one was finally selected, I was not sufficiently motivated to proceed with the work. But being a professional commercial artist, I eventually did what was required and presented the publisher with the final painting, which was approved without complaint. I was never able to forgive myself the pictorial cacophony of this piece, nor was I happy with the lack of proper tonal arrangements and absence of depth in the painting.

Above and below:
Rejected preliminary
sketches for
Children of the Lamp 7.
Pencil on paper, 2010

Final preliminary
drawing for
Children of the Lamp 7.
Pencil on paper, 2010

Children of the Lamp 7. 50x70 cm , oil on board, 2010

Personal Projects and Private Commissions

I consider myself a painter who has been deliberately lost in the world of Illustration. I see myself this way, because the pictorial aspect of painting plays an important role in my work. I also like to tell stories in my paintings. The art of story telling, though much neglected by mainstream art for many decades, is one of the most important aspects of human existence and crucially important for our survival. Illustration is all about telling stories; in that respect, I am an illustrator. I try to tell my stories as understandably as possible, but equally important to me are the pictorial qualities of my visual storytelling.

Detail from
The Rescuer

Preliminary drawing for
The Rescuer.
Pencil on paper, 2011

The Rescuer. 43x60 cm, oil on Masonite, 2011

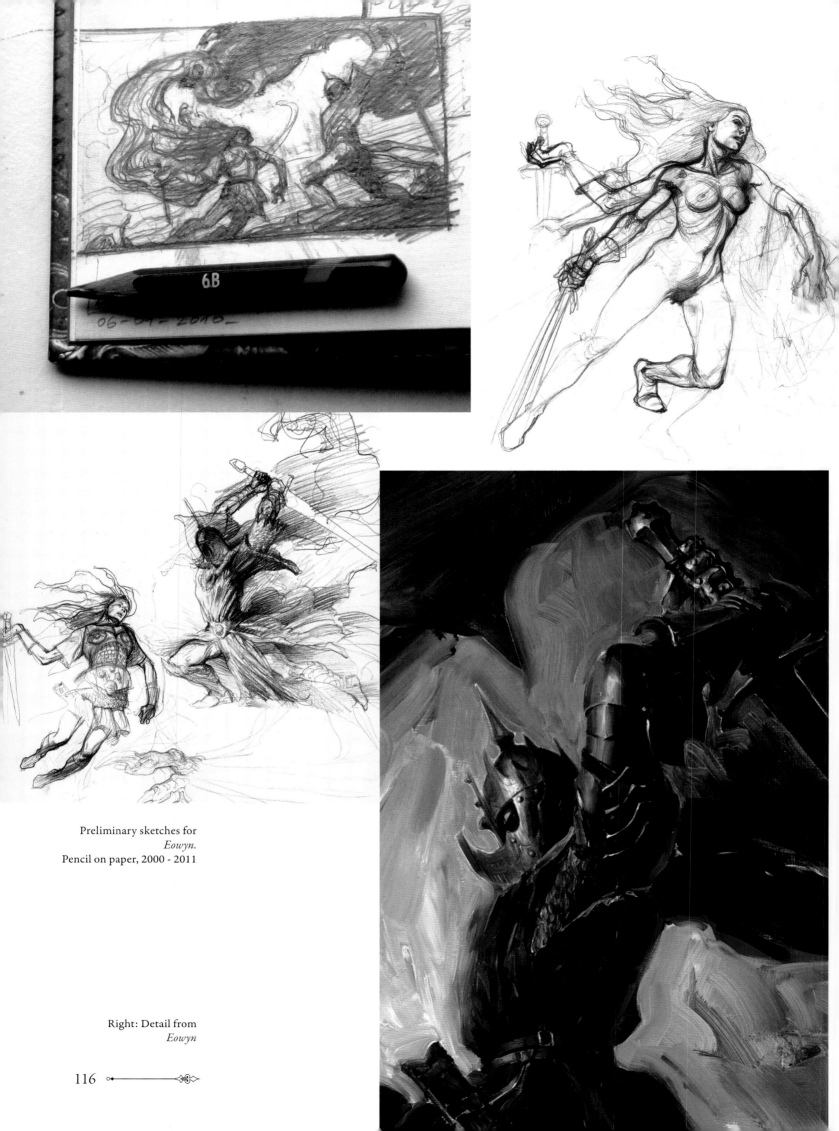

Preliminary sketches for
Eowyn.
Pencil on paper, 2000 - 2011

Right: Detail from
Eowyn

116

The painting Eowyn is an interpretation of a scene from J.R.R. Tolkien's famous book The Lord of the Rings. The genesis of this composition was very slow and gradual. I began planning this painting more than 10 years prior to its execution. From the very start I was uncertain of exactly how to handle a scene that had been illustrated so many times by numerous illustrators. Eventually I came to the conclusion to trust my instincts and do it in my own way. I was less interested to follow an exact depiction of the scene from the book, and instead focused on emphasizing the main emotion of the piece, offering many details for the sake of the whole.

Detail from
Eowyn.

Opposite far left: Detail
of the underpainting

Left: Preliminary
drawing. Pencil on paper,
2011

Below:
Dragon Race.
54x100 cm, oil on board,
2011

The requirements for this commissioned work
were clear: three women, a dragon or two, and
one or more dogs, who are all friends traveling to a
gathering.

After deciding upon the basic elements of the
composition, my main goal was to depict a situation
in which the characters interact with one another in
a specific way, and are connected by a common emotion – the joy of freedom, movement and speed.

Gandalf, 50x70 cm, oil on Masonite, 1999.

PERSONAL PROJECTS AND PRIVATE COMMISSIONS

Preliminary drawing for
Gandalf.
Pencil on paper, 1999

Gandalf is the first painting of mine in-spired by the writings of J.R.R. Tolkien. I chose not to depict any particular moment from the books, but rather to interpret the wizard's character and his function in the story. Be-ing a guardian of Life, Gandalf places himself between Good - symbolized by a door and all that is hidden behind it - and advancing Evil – represented by the horned beast. Gandalf's weapons, his earthly sword, and his magic staff embodying his supernatural powers, are crossed above his head, as if to say, 'You shall not pass!'

Shadow Comes. 50x70 cm, oil on Masonite, 1999

Detail from
Shadow Comes

Preliminary drawing for
Shadow Comes.
Pencil on paper, 1999

Preliminary drawing for
The Frost Giants.
Pencil on paper, 2012

Opposite:
The Frost Giants.
50x65 cm, oil on panel, 2012

Right:
Nordic Warrior.
Oil on paper, 2012

Preliminary sketches and
the final drawing (right)
for the painting
*Death Dealer:
Homage to Frazetta.*
Pencil on paper, 2011

I painted Death Dealer: Homage to Frazetta as a tribute to Frank Frazetta, one of the greatest masters of Fantasy Art. My intention was not to make a copy of Frazetta's world, but rather to project his character into my world and allow this character to pass through the prism of my own artistic vision. In order to find the right expression for my interpretation of the character, I did numerous preliminary sketches (previous page). The final drawing was the starting point for the next leg of my Frazetta journey, the creation of the actual painting. Here you can see the progress shots, which offer some insight into the development of this piece. For me, the essential question underlying my interpretation is: who's the bad guy here? Death Dealer or his foes?

Death Dealer: Homage to Frazetta. 55x72 cm, oil on board, 2012-2013

The Noble Dragon. 50x70 cm, oil on Masonite, 1996

The Gate Girl. 50x70 cm, oil on Masonite, 1995

PERSONAL PROJECTS AND PRIVATE COMMISSIONS

Guinevere. 50x70 cm, oil on board, 2010

132 ⋄•——◀❂▶—— PERSONAL PROJECTS AND PRIVATE COMMISSIONS

Guinevere and Lancelot.
From *King Arthur and the
Knights of the Round Table,*
22x30 cm, acrylic on
paper, 1999

In 1999, I illustrated the book King Arthur and the Knights of the Round Table for a Taiwanese publisher. One of the illustrations from this book depicts Queen Guinevere, the lovely but unfaithful wife of King Arthur, sitting by the window and waiting to be rescued by Lancelot. At first I was content with the finished piece, but later I felt there was room for improvement. At the beginning of 2010, when a Belgian collector asked me to make another painting with the same theme, I used the opportunity to improve my first version. I introduced some changes to the existing composition and painted a new Guinevere picture (previous page).

SPI Windows.
70x80 cm, oil on panel, 2009.
This was an advertising job done for an Italian company.

Above right: Preliminary drawing for one of the ghosts, pencil on paper, 2009

Right: Study of a naked giant, pencil on paper, 2010

Fine Art

Only after entering the Art Academy did I become captivated by painting. In subsequent years the need to perform this "magic" - in portraying, reflecting upon and interpreting a material world through brushstrokes - crystallized deep within me. As I grew older and more contemplative, the desire to express ideas, concepts and feelings through painting infused my work, eventually leading me to Fine Art. That I later chose to focus on Illustration Art is less important, for moving paint on canvas in order to "talk" through it remains one of the primary drives of my creative spirit.

Return of Snow-white to the Land of Abundance.
50x70 cm, oil on Masonite, 1998

Game of Chess. 60x80 cm, oil on Masonite, 2000

Remembrance. 50x70 cm, oil on canvas, 2003

The Balance. 90x120 cm, oil on canvas, 2003

The Source. 80x110 cm, oil on canvas, 2001

Detail from
The Source

Preliminary drawing for
The Exit.
Pencil on paper, 2005

The Exit. 90x120 cm, oil on canvas, 2005

Detail from
The Exit

Detail from *The Exit*

The Hunt. 70x100 cm, oil on canvas, 2000

The Family. 60x80 cm, oil on Masonite, 2001

Mother and Child. 70x100 cm, oil on canvas, 2001

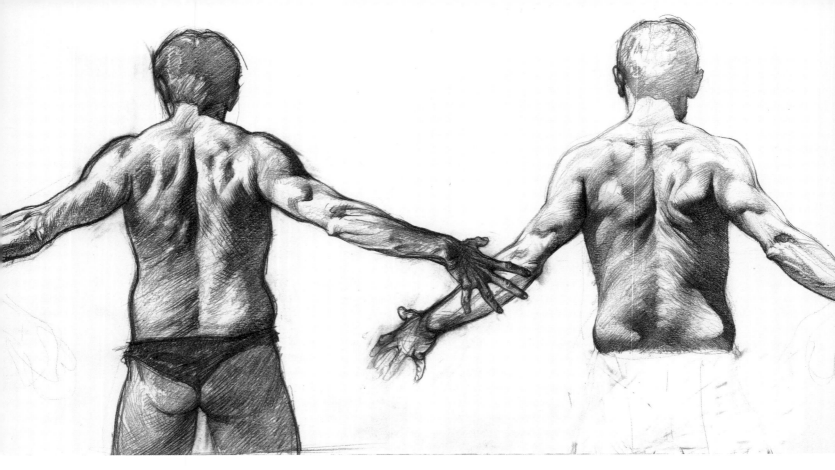

Above:
Preliminary studies,
pencil on paper, 2005

Right:
Detail from
The Dawn of the Day

The Dawn of the Day.
90x93 cm, oil on
Masonite, 2002

The paintbrush is a simple, yet powerful tool. The mark it leaves upon the canvas is wondrous – a marvel for us to behold, and a precious legacy for the people of the future. The brush stroke is a declaration of an artist's innate sensibility. As reflection of his longings, a trace of his efforts and the emanation of his unique spirit, each brush stroke is an act of creation, a mystical repetition of the initial act that created the Universe, testifying to a fundamental aspect of man's nature, his sub-creatorship in the ever-unfolding wonder of Life. These are the hidden powers of the brush stroke. Whoever understands and exercises properly this power of expression will not fail to amaze and inspire. There is much mystery hidden in a spontaneous, yet deliberate brush stroke. The embedded emotion, once frozen in this stroke, may then melt in the eyes of the spectator, releasing its flavor and fragrance. Not to be undermined by reason, these emotions penetrate deep and uncharted regions of our inner being. By reaching a level that, above all, makes us human, they strike the cords of primordial emotion, inexplicable intuition and that mysterious and eternal longing of our soul. The "signature" of the artist will be preserved in the brush stroke forever, like an echo of the past fossilized, trapped in ancient stone. Such is the power of the brush stroke.

Awakening.
90x125 cm, oil on canvas,
2006 - 2007

Right and far right:
Details from
Awakening

Resting Model 1. 36x50 cm, oil on Masonite, 2004

Resting Model 2. 40x50 cm, oil on Masonite, 2004

Anita. 40x50 cm, oil on Masonite, 2005

Serbian Still Life (Srpska mrtva priroda)
and a detail (above). 50x60 cm, oil on Masonite, 2009

Old Shoes.
30x40 cm, oil on panel,
2006

Zaanstreek light 1.
30x40 cm, oil on panel,
2006.

Autumn. 25x50 cm, oil on panel, 2007

Still Life.
70x100 cm, oil on
Masonite, 2000

Early Winter Morning 2.
27x40 cm, oil on panel,
2007

Early Spring.
15x32 cm, oil on panel,
2007